This Communication Book
Belongs to

....

Class..........................

Date:

Notes from home:

Morning Notes:

Mood:
- ☐ Great
- ☐ Ok
- ☐ Could have been better

Activities:

Toilet: Yes / No

Lunch Time Notes:

Mood:
- ☐ Great
- ☐ Ok
- ☐ Could have been better

Lunch Eaten:

Toilet: Yes / No

Afternoon Notes:

Mood:
- ☐ Great
- ☐ Ok
- ☐ Could have been better

Activities:

Toilet: Yes / No

Messages from School:

Date:

Notes from home:

Morning Notes:

Mood:
- ❏ Great
- ❏ Ok
- ❏ Could have been better

Activities:

Toilet: Yes / No

Lunch Time Notes:

Mood:
- ❏ Great
- ❏ Ok
- ❏ Could have been better

Lunch Eaten:

Toilet: Yes / No

Afternoon Notes:

Mood:
- ❏ Great
- ❏ Ok
- ❏ Could have been better

Activities:

Toilet: Yes / No

Messages from School:

Date:

Notes from home:

Morning Notes:

Mood:
- ❏ Great
- ❏ Ok
- ❏ Could have been better

Activities:

Toilet: Yes / No

Lunch Time Notes:

Mood:
- ❏ Great
- ❏ Ok
- ❏ Could have been better

Lunch Eaten:

Toilet: Yes / No

Afternoon Notes:

Mood:
- ❏ Great
- ❏ Ok
- ❏ Could have been better

Activities:

Toilet: Yes / No

Messages from School:

Date:

Notes from home:

Morning Notes:

Mood:
- ☐ Great
- ☐ Ok
- ☐ Could have been better

Activities:

Toilet: Yes / No

Lunch Time Notes:

Mood:
- ☐ Great
- ☐ Ok
- ☐ Could have been better

Lunch Eaten:

Toilet: Yes / No

Afternoon Notes:

Mood:
- ☐ Great
- ☐ Ok
- ☐ Could have been better

Activities:

Toilet: Yes / No

Messages from School:

Date:

Notes from home:

Morning Notes:

Mood:
- ❑ Great
- ❑ Ok
- ❑ Could have been better

Activities:

Toilet: Yes / No

Lunch Time Notes:

Mood:
- ❑ Great
- ❑ Ok
- ❑ Could have been better

Lunch Eaten:

Toilet: Yes / No

Afternoon Notes:

Mood:
- ❑ Great
- ❑ Ok
- ❑ Could have been better

Activities:

Toilet: Yes / No

Messages from School:

Date:

Notes from home:

Morning Notes:

Mood:
- ❏ Great
- ❏ Ok
- ❏ Could have
  been better

Activities:

Toilet: Yes / No

Lunch Time Notes:

Mood:
- ❏ Great
- ❏ Ok
- ❏ Could have
  been better

Lunch Eaten:

Toilet: Yes / No

Afternoon Notes:

Mood:
- ❏ Great
- ❏ Ok
- ❏ Could have
  been better

Activities:

Toilet: Yes / No

Messages from School:

Date:

Notes from home:

Morning Notes:

Mood:
- ☐ Great
- ☐ Ok
- ☐ Could have been better

Activities:

Toilet: Yes / No

Lunch Time Notes:

Mood:
- ☐ Great
- ☐ Ok
- ☐ Could have been better

Lunch Eaten:

Toilet: Yes / No

Afternoon Notes:

Mood:
- ☐ Great
- ☐ Ok
- ☐ Could have been better

Activities:

Toilet: Yes / No

Messages from School:

Date:

Notes from home:

Morning Notes:

Mood:
- ❑ Great
- ❑ Ok
- ❑ Could have been better

Activities:

Toilet: Yes / No

Lunch Time Notes:

Mood:
- ❑ Great
- ❑ Ok
- ❑ Could have been better

Lunch Eaten:

Toilet: Yes / No

Afternoon Notes:

Mood:
- ❑ Great
- ❑ Ok
- ❑ Could have been better

Activities:

Toilet: Yes / No

Messages from School:

Date:

Notes from home:

Morning Notes:

Mood:
- ❑ Great
- ❑ Ok
- ❑ Could have been better

Activities:

Toilet: Yes / No

Lunch Time Notes:

Mood:
- ❑ Great
- ❑ Ok
- ❑ Could have been better

Lunch Eaten:

Toilet: Yes / No

Afternoon Notes:

Mood:
- ❑ Great
- ❑ Ok
- ❑ Could have been better

Activities:

Toilet: Yes / No

Messages from School:

Date:

Notes from home:

Morning Notes:

Mood:
- ❑ Great
- ❑ Ok
- ❑ Could have been better

Activities:

Toilet: Yes / No

Lunch Time Notes:

Mood:
- ❑ Great
- ❑ Ok
- ❑ Could have been better

Lunch Eaten:

Toilet: Yes / No

Afternoon Notes:

Mood:
- ❑ Great
- ❑ Ok
- ❑ Could have been better

Activities:

Toilet: Yes / No

Messages from School:

Date:

Notes from home:

Morning Notes:

Mood:
- ❏ Great
- ❏ Ok
- ❏ Could have
    been better

Activities:

Toilet: Yes / No

Lunch Time Notes:

Mood:
- ❏ Great
- ❏ Ok
- ❏ Could have
    been better

Lunch Eaten:

Toilet: Yes / No

Afternoon Notes:

Mood:
- ❏ Great
- ❏ Ok
- ❏ Could have
    been better

Activities:

Toilet: Yes / No

Messages from School:

Date:

Notes from home:

Morning Notes:

Mood:
- ❑ Great
- ❑ Ok
- ❑ Could have been better

Activities:

Toilet: Yes / No

Lunch Time Notes:

Mood:
- ❑ Great
- ❑ Ok
- ❑ Could have been better

Lunch Eaten:

Toilet: Yes / No

Afternoon Notes:

Mood:
- ❑ Great
- ❑ Ok
- ❑ Could have been better

Activities:

Toilet: Yes / No

Messages from School:

Date:

Notes from home:

Morning Notes:

Mood:
- ❑ Great
- ❑ Ok
- ❑ Could have been better

Activities:

Toilet: Yes / No

Lunch Time Notes:

Mood:
- ❑ Great
- ❑ Ok
- ❑ Could have been better

Lunch Eaten:

Toilet: Yes / No

Afternoon Notes:

Mood:
- ❑ Great
- ❑ Ok
- ❑ Could have been better

Activities:

Toilet: Yes / No

Messages from School:

Date:

Notes from home:

Morning Notes:

Mood:
- ❑ Great
- ❑ Ok
- ❑ Could have been better

Activities:

Toilet: Yes / No

Lunch Time Notes:

Mood:
- ❑ Great
- ❑ Ok
- ❑ Could have been better

Lunch Eaten:

Toilet: Yes / No

Afternoon Notes:

Mood:
- ❑ Great
- ❑ Ok
- ❑ Could have been better

Activities:

Toilet: Yes / No

Messages from School:

Date:

Notes from home:

Morning Notes:

Mood:
- ☐ Great
- ☐ Ok
- ☐ Could have been better

Activities:

Toilet: Yes / No

Lunch Time Notes:

Mood:
- ☐ Great
- ☐ Ok
- ☐ Could have been better

Lunch Eaten:

Toilet: Yes / No

Afternoon Notes:

Mood:
- ☐ Great
- ☐ Ok
- ☐ Could have been better

Activities:

Toilet: Yes / No

Messages from School:

Date:

Notes from home:

Morning Notes:

Mood:
- ❑ Great
- ❑ Ok
- ❑ Could have
  been better

Activities:

Toilet: Yes / No

Lunch Time Notes:

Mood:
- ❑ Great
- ❑ Ok
- ❑ Could have
  been better

Lunch Eaten:

Toilet: Yes / No

Afternoon Notes:

Mood:
- ❑ Great
- ❑ Ok
- ❑ Could have
  been better

Activities:

Toilet: Yes / No

Messages from School:

Date:

Notes from home:

Morning Notes:

Mood:
- ☐ Great
- ☐ Ok
- ☐ Could have been better

Activities:

Toilet: Yes / No

Lunch Time Notes:

Mood:
- ☐ Great
- ☐ Ok
- ☐ Could have been better

Lunch Eaten:

Toilet: Yes / No

Afternoon Notes:

Mood:
- ☐ Great
- ☐ Ok
- ☐ Could have been better

Activities:

Toilet: Yes / No

Messages from School:

Date:

Notes from home:

Morning Notes:

Mood:
- ❑ Great
- ❑ Ok
- ❑ Could have been better

Activities:

Toilet: Yes / No

Lunch Time Notes:

Mood:
- ❑ Great
- ❑ Ok
- ❑ Could have been better

Lunch Eaten:

Toilet: Yes / No

Afternoon Notes:

Mood:
- ❑ Great
- ❑ Ok
- ❑ Could have been better

Activities:

Toilet: Yes / No

Messages from School:

Date:

Notes from home:

Morning Notes:

Mood:
- ❑ Great
- ❑ Ok
- ❑ Could have been better

Activities:

Toilet: Yes / No

Lunch Time Notes:

Mood:
- ❑ Great
- ❑ Ok
- ❑ Could have been better

Lunch Eaten:

Toilet: Yes / No

Afternoon Notes:

Mood:
- ❑ Great
- ❑ Ok
- ❑ Could have been better

Activities:

Toilet: Yes / No

Messages from School:

Date:

Notes from home:

Morning Notes:

Mood:
- ❑ Great
- ❑ Ok
- ❑ Could have
  been better

Activities:

Toilet: Yes / No

Lunch Time Notes:

Mood:
- ❑ Great
- ❑ Ok
- ❑ Could have
  been better

Lunch Eaten:

Toilet: Yes / No

Afternoon Notes:

Mood:
- ❑ Great
- ❑ Ok
- ❑ Could have
  been better

Activities:

Toilet: Yes / No

Messages from School:

Date:

Notes from home:

Morning Notes:

Mood:
- ❑ Great
- ❑ Ok
- ❑ Could have been better

Activities:

Toilet: Yes / No

Lunch Time Notes:

Mood:
- ❑ Great
- ❑ Ok
- ❑ Could have been better

Lunch Eaten:

Toilet: Yes / No

Afternoon Notes:

Mood:
- ❑ Great
- ❑ Ok
- ❑ Could have been better

Activities:

Toilet: Yes / No

Messages from School:

Date:

Notes from home:

Morning Notes:

Mood:
- ☐ Great
- ☐ Ok
- ☐ Could have
  been better

Activities:

Toilet: Yes / No

Lunch Time Notes:

Mood:
- ☐ Great
- ☐ Ok
- ☐ Could have
  been better

Lunch Eaten:

Toilet: Yes / No

Afternoon Notes:

Mood:
- ☐ Great
- ☐ Ok
- ☐ Could have
  been better

Activities:

Toilet: Yes / No

Messages from School:

Date:

Notes from home:

Morning Notes:

Mood:
- ❑ Great
- ❑ Ok
- ❑ Could have been better

Activities:

Toilet: Yes / No

Lunch Time Notes:

Mood:
- ❑ Great
- ❑ Ok
- ❑ Could have been better

Lunch Eaten:

Toilet: Yes / No

Afternoon Notes:

Mood:
- ❑ Great
- ❑ Ok
- ❑ Could have been better

Activities:

Toilet: Yes / No

Messages from School:

Date:

Notes from home:

Morning Notes:

Mood:
- ❏ Great
- ❏ Ok
- ❏ Could have been better

Activities:

Toilet: Yes / No

Lunch Time Notes:

Mood:
- ❏ Great
- ❏ Ok
- ❏ Could have been better

Lunch Eaten:

Toilet: Yes / No

Afternoon Notes:

Mood:
- ❏ Great
- ❏ Ok
- ❏ Could have been better

Activities:

Toilet: Yes / No

Messages from School:

Date:

Notes from home:

Morning Notes:

Mood:
- ❑ Great
- ❑ Ok
- ❑ Could have been better

Activities:

Toilet: Yes / No

Lunch Time Notes:

Mood:
- ❑ Great
- ❑ Ok
- ❑ Could have been better

Lunch Eaten:

Toilet: Yes / No

Afternoon Notes:

Mood:
- ❑ Great
- ❑ Ok
- ❑ Could have been better

Activities:

Toilet: Yes / No

Messages from School:

Date:

Notes from home:

Morning Notes:

Mood:
- ❑ Great
- ❑ Ok
- ❑ Could have been better

Activities:

Toilet: Yes / No

Lunch Time Notes:

Mood:
- ❑ Great
- ❑ Ok
- ❑ Could have been better

Lunch Eaten:

Toilet: Yes / No

Afternoon Notes:

Mood:
- ❑ Great
- ❑ Ok
- ❑ Could have been better

Activities:

Toilet: Yes / No

Messages from School:

Date:

Notes from home:

Morning Notes:

Mood:
- ❑ Great
- ❑ Ok
- ❑ Could have been better

Activities:

Toilet: Yes / No

Lunch Time Notes:

Mood:
- ❑ Great
- ❑ Ok
- ❑ Could have been better

Lunch Eaten:

Toilet: Yes / No

Afternoon Notes:

Mood:
- ❑ Great
- ❑ Ok
- ❑ Could have been better

Activities:

Toilet: Yes / No

Messages from School:

Date:

Notes from home:

Morning Notes:

Mood:
- ❑ Great
- ❑ Ok
- ❑ Could have been better

Activities:

Toilet: Yes / No

Lunch Time Notes:

Mood:
- ❑ Great
- ❑ Ok
- ❑ Could have been better

Lunch Eaten:

Toilet: Yes / No

Afternoon Notes:

Mood:
- ❑ Great
- ❑ Ok
- ❑ Could have been better

Activities:

Toilet: Yes / No

Messages from School:

Date:

Notes from home:

Morning Notes:

Mood:
- ☐ Great
- ☐ Ok
- ☐ Could have
  been better

Activities:

Toilet: Yes / No

Lunch Time Notes:

Mood:
- ☐ Great
- ☐ Ok
- ☐ Could have
  been better

Lunch Eaten:

Toilet: Yes / No

Afternoon Notes:

Mood:
- ☐ Great
- ☐ Ok
- ☐ Could have
  been better

Activities:

Toilet: Yes / No

Messages from School:

Date:

Notes from home:

Morning Notes:

Mood:
- [ ] Great
- [ ] Ok
- [ ] Could have been better

Activities:

Toilet: Yes / No

Lunch Time Notes:

Mood:
- [ ] Great
- [ ] Ok
- [ ] Could have been better

Lunch Eaten:

Toilet: Yes / No

Afternoon Notes:

Mood:
- [ ] Great
- [ ] Ok
- [ ] Could have been better

Activities:

Toilet: Yes / No

Messages from School:

Date:

Notes from home:

Morning Notes:

Mood:
- ❑ Great
- ❑ Ok
- ❑ Could have been better

Activities:

Toilet: Yes / No

Lunch Time Notes:

Mood:
- ❑ Great
- ❑ Ok
- ❑ Could have been better

Lunch Eaten:

Toilet: Yes / No

Afternoon Notes:

Mood:
- ❑ Great
- ❑ Ok
- ❑ Could have been better

Activities:

Toilet: Yes / No

Messages from School:

Date:

Notes from home:

Morning Notes:

Mood:
- ☐ Great
- ☐ Ok
- ☐ Could have
  been better

Activities:

Toilet: Yes / No

Lunch Time Notes:

Mood:
- ☐ Great
- ☐ Ok
- ☐ Could have
  been better

Lunch Eaten:

Toilet: Yes / No

Afternoon Notes:

Mood:
- ☐ Great
- ☐ Ok
- ☐ Could have
  been better

Activities:

Toilet: Yes / No

Messages from School:

Date:

Notes from home:

Morning Notes:

Mood:
- ❏ Great
- ❏ Ok
- ❏ Could have been better

Activities:

Toilet: Yes / No

Lunch Time Notes:

Mood:
- ❏ Great
- ❏ Ok
- ❏ Could have been better

Lunch Eaten:

Toilet: Yes / No

Afternoon Notes:

Mood:
- ❏ Great
- ❏ Ok
- ❏ Could have been better

Activities:

Toilet: Yes / No

Messages from School:

Date:

Notes from home:

Morning Notes:

Mood:
❑ Great
❑ Ok
❑ Could have
  been better

Activities:

Toilet: Yes / No

Lunch Time Notes:

Mood:
❑ Great
❑ Ok
❑ Could have
  been better

Lunch Eaten:

Toilet: Yes / No

Afternoon Notes:

Mood:
❑ Great
❑ Ok
❑ Could have
  been better

Activities:

Toilet: Yes / No

Messages from School:

Date:

Notes from home:

Morning Notes:

Mood:
- ❑ Great
- ❑ Ok
- ❑ Could have
  been better

Activities:

Toilet: Yes / No

Lunch Time Notes:

Mood:
- ❑ Great
- ❑ Ok
- ❑ Could have
  been better

Lunch Eaten:

Toilet: Yes / No

Afternoon Notes:

Mood:
- ❑ Great
- ❑ Ok
- ❑ Could have
  been better

Activities:

Toilet: Yes / No

Messages from School:

Date:

Notes from home:

Morning Notes:

Mood:
- ❑ Great
- ❑ Ok
- ❑ Could have
  been better

Activities:

Toilet: Yes / No

Lunch Time Notes:

Mood:
- ❑ Great
- ❑ Ok
- ❑ Could have
  been better

Lunch Eaten:

Toilet: Yes / No

Afternoon Notes:

Mood:
- ❑ Great
- ❑ Ok
- ❑ Could have
  been better

Activities:

Toilet: Yes / No

Messages from School:

Date:

Notes from home:

Morning Notes:

Mood:
- ❑ Great
- ❑ Ok
- ❑ Could have
     been better

Activities:

Toilet: Yes / No

Lunch Time Notes:

Mood:
- ❑ Great
- ❑ Ok
- ❑ Could have
     been better

Lunch Eaten:

Toilet: Yes / No

Afternoon Notes:

Mood:
- ❑ Great
- ❑ Ok
- ❑ Could have
     been better

Activities:

Toilet: Yes / No

Messages from School:

Date:

Notes from home:

Morning Notes:

Mood:
- ❑ Great
- ❑ Ok
- ❑ Could have been better

Activities:

Toilet: Yes / No

Lunch Time Notes:

Mood:
- ❑ Great
- ❑ Ok
- ❑ Could have been better

Lunch Eaten:

Toilet: Yes / No

Afternoon Notes:

Mood:
- ❑ Great
- ❑ Ok
- ❑ Could have been better

Activities:

Toilet: Yes / No

Messages from School:

Date:

Notes from home:

Morning Notes:

Mood:
- ❑ Great
- ❑ Ok
- ❑ Could have been better

Activities:

Toilet: Yes / No

Lunch Time Notes:

Mood:
- ❑ Great
- ❑ Ok
- ❑ Could have been better

Lunch Eaten:

Toilet: Yes / No

Afternoon Notes:

Mood:
- ❑ Great
- ❑ Ok
- ❑ Could have been better

Activities:

Toilet: Yes / No

Messages from School:

Date:

Notes from home:

Morning Notes:

Mood:
- ❑ Great
- ❑ Ok
- ❑ Could have
  been better

Activities:

Toilet: Yes / No

Lunch Time Notes:

Mood:
- ❑ Great
- ❑ Ok
- ❑ Could have
  been better

Lunch Eaten:

Toilet: Yes / No

Afternoon Notes:

Mood:
- ❑ Great
- ❑ Ok
- ❑ Could have
  been better

Activities:

Toilet: Yes / No

Messages from School:

Date:

Notes from home:

Morning Notes:

Mood:
- ❑ Great
- ❑ Ok
- ❑ Could have been better

Activities:

Toilet: Yes / No

Lunch Time Notes:

Mood:
- ❑ Great
- ❑ Ok
- ❑ Could have been better

Lunch Eaten:

Toilet: Yes / No

Afternoon Notes:

Mood:
- ❑ Great
- ❑ Ok
- ❑ Could have been better

Activities:

Toilet: Yes / No

Messages from School:

Date:

Notes from home:

Morning Notes:

Mood:
- ❑ Great
- ❑ Ok
- ❑ Could have been better

Activities:

Toilet: Yes / No

Lunch Time Notes:

Mood:
- ❑ Great
- ❑ Ok
- ❑ Could have been better

Lunch Eaten:

Toilet: Yes / No

Afternoon Notes:

Mood:
- ❑ Great
- ❑ Ok
- ❑ Could have been better

Activities:

Toilet: Yes / No

Messages from School:

Date:

Notes from home:

Morning Notes:

Mood:
- ☐ Great
- ☐ Ok
- ☐ Could have been better

Activities:

Toilet: Yes / No

Lunch Time Notes:

Mood:
- ☐ Great
- ☐ Ok
- ☐ Could have been better

Lunch Eaten:

Toilet: Yes / No

Afternoon Notes:

Mood:
- ☐ Great
- ☐ Ok
- ☐ Could have been better

Activities:

Toilet: Yes / No

Messages from School:

Date:

Notes from home:

Morning Notes:

Mood:
☐ Great
☐ Ok
☐ Could have
   been better

Activities:

Toilet: Yes / No

Lunch Time Notes:

Mood:
☐ Great
☐ Ok
☐ Could have
   been better

Lunch Eaten:

Toilet: Yes / No

Afternoon Notes:

Mood:
☐ Great
☐ Ok
☐ Could have
   been better

Activities:

Toilet: Yes / No

Messages from School:

Date:

Notes from home:

Morning Notes:

Mood:
- ❑ Great
- ❑ Ok
- ❑ Could have been better

Activities:

Toilet: Yes / No

Lunch Time Notes:

Mood:
- ❑ Great
- ❑ Ok
- ❑ Could have been better

Lunch Eaten:

Toilet: Yes / No

Afternoon Notes:

Mood:
- ❑ Great
- ❑ Ok
- ❑ Could have been better

Activities:

Toilet: Yes / No

Messages from School:

Date:

Notes from home:

Morning Notes:

Mood:
- ❑ Great
- ❑ Ok
- ❑ Could have been better

Activities:

Toilet: Yes / No

Lunch Time Notes:

Mood:
- ❑ Great
- ❑ Ok
- ❑ Could have been better

Lunch Eaten:

Toilet: Yes / No

Afternoon Notes:

Mood:
- ❑ Great
- ❑ Ok
- ❑ Could have been better

Activities:

Toilet: Yes / No

Messages from School:

Date:

Notes from home:

Morning Notes:

Mood:
❑ Great
❑ Ok
❑ Could have
   been better

Activities:

Toilet: Yes / No

Lunch Time Notes:

Mood:
❑ Great
❑ Ok
❑ Could have
   been better

Lunch Eaten:

Toilet: Yes / No

Afternoon Notes:

Mood:
❑ Great
❑ Ok
❑ Could have
   been better

Activities:

Toilet: Yes / No

Messages from School:

Date:

Notes from home:

Morning Notes:

Mood:
- ❑ Great
- ❑ Ok
- ❑ Could have been better

Activities:

Toilet: Yes / No

Lunch Time Notes:

Mood:
- ❑ Great
- ❑ Ok
- ❑ Could have been better

Lunch Eaten:

Toilet: Yes / No

Afternoon Notes:

Mood:
- ❑ Great
- ❑ Ok
- ❑ Could have been better

Activities:

Toilet: Yes / No

Messages from School:

Date:

Notes from home:

Morning Notes:

Mood:
❑ Great
❑ Ok
❑ Could have
been better

Activities:

Toilet: Yes / No

Lunch Time Notes:

Mood:
❑ Great
❑ Ok
❑ Could have
been better

Lunch Eaten:

Toilet: Yes / No

Afternoon Notes:

Mood:
❑ Great
❑ Ok
❑ Could have
been better

Activities:

Toilet: Yes / No

Messages from School:

Date:

Notes from home:

Morning Notes:

Mood:
- ❑ Great
- ❑ Ok
- ❑ Could have
  been better

Activities:

Toilet: Yes / No

Lunch Time Notes:

Mood:
- ❑ Great
- ❑ Ok
- ❑ Could have
  been better

Lunch Eaten:

Toilet: Yes / No

Afternoon Notes:

Mood:
- ❑ Great
- ❑ Ok
- ❑ Could have
  been better

Activities:

Toilet: Yes / No

Messages from School:

Date:

Notes from home:

Morning Notes:

Mood:
- ❑ Great
- ❑ Ok
- ❑ Could have been better

Activities:

Toilet: Yes / No

Lunch Time Notes:

Mood:
- ❑ Great
- ❑ Ok
- ❑ Could have been better

Lunch Eaten:

Toilet: Yes / No

Afternoon Notes:

Mood:
- ❑ Great
- ❑ Ok
- ❑ Could have been better

Activities:

Toilet: Yes / No

Messages from School:

Date:

Notes from home:

Morning Notes:

Mood:
- ❑ Great
- ❑ Ok
- ❑ Could have been better

Activities:

Toilet: Yes / No

Lunch Time Notes:

Mood:
- ❑ Great
- ❑ Ok
- ❑ Could have been better

Lunch Eaten:

Toilet: Yes / No

Afternoon Notes:

Mood:
- ❑ Great
- ❑ Ok
- ❑ Could have been better

Activities:

Toilet: Yes / No

Messages from School:

Date:

Notes from home:

Morning Notes:

Mood:
- ❑ Great
- ❑ Ok
- ❑ Could have been better

Activities:

Toilet: Yes / No

Lunch Time Notes:

Mood:
- ❑ Great
- ❑ Ok
- ❑ Could have been better

Lunch Eaten:

Toilet: Yes / No

Afternoon Notes:

Mood:
- ❑ Great
- ❑ Ok
- ❑ Could have been better

Activities:

Toilet: Yes / No

Messages from School:

Date:

Notes from home:

Morning Notes:

Mood:
- ❑ Great
- ❑ Ok
- ❑ Could have
  been better

Activities:

Toilet: Yes / No

Lunch Time Notes:

Mood:
- ❑ Great
- ❑ Ok
- ❑ Could have
  been better

Lunch Eaten:

Toilet: Yes / No

Afternoon Notes:

Mood:
- ❑ Great
- ❑ Ok
- ❑ Could have
  been better

Activities:

Toilet: Yes / No

Messages from School:

Date:

Notes from home:

Morning Notes:

Mood:
- ❑ Great
- ❑ Ok
- ❑ Could have been better

Activities:

Toilet: Yes / No

Lunch Time Notes:

Mood:
- ❑ Great
- ❑ Ok
- ❑ Could have been better

Lunch Eaten:

Toilet: Yes / No

Afternoon Notes:

Mood:
- ❑ Great
- ❑ Ok
- ❑ Could have been better

Activities:

Toilet: Yes / No

Messages from School:

Date:

Notes from home:

Morning Notes:

Mood:
- ❑ Great
- ❑ Ok
- ❑ Could have
  been better

Activities:

Toilet: Yes / No

Lunch Time Notes:

Mood:
- ❑ Great
- ❑ Ok
- ❑ Could have
  been better

Lunch Eaten:

Toilet: Yes / No

Afternoon Notes:

Mood:
- ❑ Great
- ❑ Ok
- ❑ Could have
  been better

Activities:

Toilet: Yes / No

Messages from School:

Date:

Notes from home:

Morning Notes:

Mood:
- ☐ Great
- ☐ Ok
- ☐ Could have been better

Activities:

Toilet: Yes / No

Lunch Time Notes:

Mood:
- ☐ Great
- ☐ Ok
- ☐ Could have been better

Lunch Eaten:

Toilet: Yes / No

Afternoon Notes:

Mood:
- ☐ Great
- ☐ Ok
- ☐ Could have been better

Activities:

Toilet: Yes / No

Messages from School:

Date:

Notes from home:

Morning Notes:

Mood:
- ❏ Great
- ❏ Ok
- ❏ Could have been better

Activities:

Toilet: Yes / No

Lunch Time Notes:

Mood:
- ❏ Great
- ❏ Ok
- ❏ Could have been better

Lunch Eaten:

Toilet: Yes / No

Afternoon Notes:

Mood:
- ❏ Great
- ❏ Ok
- ❏ Could have been better

Activities:

Toilet: Yes / No

Messages from School:

Date:

Notes from home:

Morning Notes:

Mood:
- ❑ Great
- ❑ Ok
- ❑ Could have been better

Activities:

Toilet: Yes / No

Lunch Time Notes:

Mood:
- ❑ Great
- ❑ Ok
- ❑ Could have been better

Lunch Eaten:

Toilet: Yes / No

Afternoon Notes:

Mood:
- ❑ Great
- ❑ Ok
- ❑ Could have been better

Activities:

Toilet: Yes / No

Messages from School:

Date:

Notes from home:

Morning Notes:

Mood:
❑ Great
❑ Ok
❑ Could have
   been better

Activities:

Toilet: Yes / No

Lunch Time Notes:

Mood:
❑ Great
❑ Ok
❑ Could have
   been better

Lunch Eaten:

Toilet: Yes / No

Afternoon Notes:

Mood:
❑ Great
❑ Ok
❑ Could have
   been better

Activities:

Toilet: Yes / No

Messages from School:

Date:

Notes from home:

Morning Notes:

Mood:
- ❑ Great
- ❑ Ok
- ❑ Could have been better

Activities:

Toilet: Yes / No

Lunch Time Notes:

Mood:
- ❑ Great
- ❑ Ok
- ❑ Could have been better

Lunch Eaten:

Toilet: Yes / No

Afternoon Notes:

Mood:
- ❑ Great
- ❑ Ok
- ❑ Could have been better

Activities:

Toilet: Yes / No

Messages from School:

Date:

Notes from home:

Morning Notes:

Mood:
- ❑ Great
- ❑ Ok
- ❑ Could have been better

Activities:

Toilet: Yes / No

Lunch Time Notes:

Mood:
- ❑ Great
- ❑ Ok
- ❑ Could have been better

Lunch Eaten:

Toilet: Yes / No

Afternoon Notes:

Mood:
- ❑ Great
- ❑ Ok
- ❑ Could have been better

Activities:

Toilet: Yes / No

Messages from School:

Date:

Notes from home:

Morning Notes:

Mood:
- ❏ Great
- ❏ Ok
- ❏ Could have been better

Activities:

Toilet: Yes / No

Lunch Time Notes:

Mood:
- ❏ Great
- ❏ Ok
- ❏ Could have been better

Lunch Eaten:

Toilet: Yes / No

Afternoon Notes:

Mood:
- ❏ Great
- ❏ Ok
- ❏ Could have been better

Activities:

Toilet: Yes / No

Messages from School:

Date:

Notes from home:

Morning Notes:

Mood:
- ❑ Great
- ❑ Ok
- ❑ Could have been better

Activities:

Toilet: Yes / No

Lunch Time Notes:

Mood:
- ❑ Great
- ❑ Ok
- ❑ Could have been better

Lunch Eaten:

Toilet: Yes / No

Afternoon Notes:

Mood:
- ❑ Great
- ❑ Ok
- ❑ Could have been better

Activities:

Toilet: Yes / No

Messages from School:

Date:

Notes from home:

Morning Notes:

Mood:
- ❑ Great
- ❑ Ok
- ❑ Could have been better

Activities:

Toilet: Yes / No

Lunch Time Notes:

Mood:
- ❑ Great
- ❑ Ok
- ❑ Could have been better

Lunch Eaten:

Toilet: Yes / No

Afternoon Notes:

Mood:
- ❑ Great
- ❑ Ok
- ❑ Could have been better

Activities:

Toilet: Yes / No

Messages from School:

Date:

Notes from home:

Morning Notes:

Mood:
- ❑ Great
- ❑ Ok
- ❑ Could have been better

Activities:

Toilet: Yes / No

Lunch Time Notes:

Mood:
- ❑ Great
- ❑ Ok
- ❑ Could have been better

Lunch Eaten:

Toilet: Yes / No

Afternoon Notes:

Mood:
- ❑ Great
- ❑ Ok
- ❑ Could have been better

Activities:

Toilet: Yes / No

Messages from School:

Date:

Notes from home:

Morning Notes:

Mood:
- ☐ Great
- ☐ Ok
- ☐ Could have been better

Activities:

Toilet: Yes / No

Lunch Time Notes:

Mood:
- ☐ Great
- ☐ Ok
- ☐ Could have been better

Lunch Eaten:

Toilet: Yes / No

Afternoon Notes:

Mood:
- ☐ Great
- ☐ Ok
- ☐ Could have been better

Activities:

Toilet: Yes / No

Messages from School:

Date:

Notes from home:

Morning Notes:

Mood:
- ❑ Great
- ❑ Ok
- ❑ Could have
  been better

Activities:

Toilet: Yes / No

Lunch Time Notes:

Mood:
- ❑ Great
- ❑ Ok
- ❑ Could have
  been better

Lunch Eaten:

Toilet: Yes / No

Afternoon Notes:

Mood:
- ❑ Great
- ❑ Ok
- ❑ Could have
  been better

Activities:

Toilet: Yes / No

Messages from School:

Date:

Notes from home:

Morning Notes:

Mood:
- ❑ Great
- ❑ Ok
- ❑ Could have been better

Activities:

Toilet: Yes / No

Lunch Time Notes:

Mood:
- ❑ Great
- ❑ Ok
- ❑ Could have been better

Lunch Eaten:

Toilet: Yes / No

Afternoon Notes:

Mood:
- ❑ Great
- ❑ Ok
- ❑ Could have been better

Activities:

Toilet: Yes / No

Messages from School:

Date:

Notes from home:

Morning Notes:

Mood:
- ☐ Great
- ☐ Ok
- ☐ Could have been better

Activities:

Toilet: Yes / No

Lunch Time Notes:

Mood:
- ☐ Great
- ☐ Ok
- ☐ Could have been better

Lunch Eaten:

Toilet: Yes / No

Afternoon Notes:

Mood:
- ☐ Great
- ☐ Ok
- ☐ Could have been better

Activities:

Toilet: Yes / No

Messages from School:

Date:

Notes from home:

Morning Notes:

Mood:
- ❑ Great
- ❑ Ok
- ❑ Could have been better

Activities:

Toilet: Yes / No

Lunch Time Notes:

Mood:
- ❑ Great
- ❑ Ok
- ❑ Could have been better

Lunch Eaten:

Toilet: Yes / No

Afternoon Notes:

Mood:
- ❑ Great
- ❑ Ok
- ❑ Could have been better

Activities:

Toilet: Yes / No

Messages from School:

Date:

Notes from home:

Morning Notes:

Mood:
- ❑ Great
- ❑ Ok
- ❑ Could have been better

Activities:

Toilet: Yes / No

Lunch Time Notes:

Mood:
- ❑ Great
- ❑ Ok
- ❑ Could have been better

Lunch Eaten:

Toilet: Yes / No

Afternoon Notes:

Mood:
- ❑ Great
- ❑ Ok
- ❑ Could have been better

Activities:

Toilet: Yes / No

Messages from School:

Date:

Notes from home:

Morning Notes:

Mood:
- ❑ Great
- ❑ Ok
- ❑ Could have been better

Activities:

Toilet: Yes / No

Lunch Time Notes:

Mood:
- ❑ Great
- ❑ Ok
- ❑ Could have been better

Lunch Eaten:

Toilet: Yes / No

Afternoon Notes:

Mood:
- ❑ Great
- ❑ Ok
- ❑ Could have been better

Activities:

Toilet: Yes / No

Messages from School:

Date:

Notes from home:

Morning Notes:

Mood:
- ❑ Great
- ❑ Ok
- ❑ Could have been better

Activities:

Toilet: Yes / No

Lunch Time Notes:

Mood:
- ❑ Great
- ❑ Ok
- ❑ Could have been better

Lunch Eaten:

Toilet: Yes / No

Afternoon Notes:

Mood:
- ❑ Great
- ❑ Ok
- ❑ Could have been better

Activities:

Toilet: Yes / No

Messages from School:

Date:

Notes from home:

Morning Notes:

Mood:
- ☐ Great
- ☐ Ok
- ☐ Could have been better

Activities:

Toilet: Yes / No

Lunch Time Notes:

Mood:
- ☐ Great
- ☐ Ok
- ☐ Could have been better

Lunch Eaten:

Toilet: Yes / No

Afternoon Notes:

Mood:
- ☐ Great
- ☐ Ok
- ☐ Could have been better

Activities:

Toilet: Yes / No

Messages from School:

Date:

Notes from home:

Morning Notes:

Mood:
- ❑ Great
- ❑ Ok
- ❑ Could have been better

Activities:

Toilet: Yes / No

Lunch Time Notes:

Mood:
- ❑ Great
- ❑ Ok
- ❑ Could have been better

Lunch Eaten:

Toilet: Yes / No

Afternoon Notes:

Mood:
- ❑ Great
- ❑ Ok
- ❑ Could have been better

Activities:

Toilet: Yes / No

Messages from School:

Date:

Notes from home:

Morning Notes:

Mood:
- ❏ Great
- ❏ Ok
- ❏ Could have been better

Activities:

Toilet: Yes / No

Lunch Time Notes:

Mood:
- ❏ Great
- ❏ Ok
- ❏ Could have been better

Lunch Eaten:

Toilet: Yes / No

Afternoon Notes:

Mood:
- ❏ Great
- ❏ Ok
- ❏ Could have been better

Activities:

Toilet: Yes / No

Messages from School:

Date:

Notes from home:

Morning Notes:

Mood:
❑ Great
❑ Ok
❑ Could have
  been better

Activities:

Toilet: Yes / No

Lunch Time Notes:

Mood:
❑ Great
❑ Ok
❑ Could have
  been better

Lunch Eaten:

Toilet: Yes / No

Afternoon Notes:

Mood:
❑ Great
❑ Ok
❑ Could have
  been better

Activities:

Toilet: Yes / No

Messages from School:

Date:

Notes from home:

Morning Notes:

Mood:
- ❑ Great
- ❑ Ok
- ❑ Could have been better

Activities:

Toilet: Yes / No

Lunch Time Notes:

Mood:
- ❑ Great
- ❑ Ok
- ❑ Could have been better

Lunch Eaten:

Toilet: Yes / No

Afternoon Notes:

Mood:
- ❑ Great
- ❑ Ok
- ❑ Could have been better

Activities:

Toilet: Yes / No

Messages from School:

Date:

Notes from home:

Morning Notes:

Mood:
- ❑ Great
- ❑ Ok
- ❑ Could have been better

Activities:

Toilet: Yes / No

Lunch Time Notes:

Mood:
- ❑ Great
- ❑ Ok
- ❑ Could have been better

Lunch Eaten:

Toilet: Yes / No

Afternoon Notes:

Mood:
- ❑ Great
- ❑ Ok
- ❑ Could have been better

Activities:

Toilet: Yes / No

Messages from School:

Date:

Notes from home:

Morning Notes:

Mood:
- ❑ Great
- ❑ Ok
- ❑ Could have been better

Activities:

Toilet: Yes / No

Lunch Time Notes:

Mood:
- ❑ Great
- ❑ Ok
- ❑ Could have been better

Lunch Eaten:

Toilet: Yes / No

Afternoon Notes:

Mood:
- ❑ Great
- ❑ Ok
- ❑ Could have been better

Activities:

Toilet: Yes / No

Messages from School:

Date:

Notes from home:

Morning Notes:

Mood:
- ❑ Great
- ❑ Ok
- ❑ Could have been better

Activities:

Toilet: Yes / No

Lunch Time Notes:

Mood:
- ❑ Great
- ❑ Ok
- ❑ Could have been better

Lunch Eaten:

Toilet: Yes / No

Afternoon Notes:

Mood:
- ❑ Great
- ❑ Ok
- ❑ Could have been better

Activities:

Toilet: Yes / No

Messages from School:

Date:

Notes from home:

Morning Notes:

Mood:
- ❑ Great
- ❑ Ok
- ❑ Could have
  been better

Activities:

Toilet: Yes / No

Lunch Time Notes:

Mood:
- ❑ Great
- ❑ Ok
- ❑ Could have
  been better

Lunch Eaten:

Toilet: Yes / No

Afternoon Notes:

Mood:
- ❑ Great
- ❑ Ok
- ❑ Could have
  been better

Activities:

Toilet: Yes / No

Messages from School:

Date:

Notes from home:

Morning Notes:

Mood:
- ☐ Great
- ☐ Ok
- ☐ Could have
  been better

Activities:

Toilet: Yes / No

Lunch Time Notes:

Mood:
- ☐ Great
- ☐ Ok
- ☐ Could have
  been better

Lunch Eaten:

Toilet: Yes / No

Afternoon Notes:

Mood:
- ☐ Great
- ☐ Ok
- ☐ Could have
  been better

Activities:

Toilet: Yes / No

Messages from School:

Date:

Notes from home:

Morning Notes:

Mood:
- ❑ Great
- ❑ Ok
- ❑ Could have been better

Activities:

Toilet: Yes / No

Lunch Time Notes:

Mood:
- ❑ Great
- ❑ Ok
- ❑ Could have been better

Lunch Eaten:

Toilet: Yes / No

Afternoon Notes:

Mood:
- ❑ Great
- ❑ Ok
- ❑ Could have been better

Activities:

Toilet: Yes / No

Messages from School:

Date:

Notes from home:

Morning Notes:

Mood:
- ❑ Great
- ❑ Ok
- ❑ Could have been better

Activities:

Toilet: Yes / No

Lunch Time Notes:

Mood:
- ❑ Great
- ❑ Ok
- ❑ Could have been better

Lunch Eaten:

Toilet: Yes / No

Afternoon Notes:

Mood:
- ❑ Great
- ❑ Ok
- ❑ Could have been better

Activities:

Toilet: Yes / No

Messages from School:

Date:

Notes from home:

Morning Notes:

Mood:
- ❑ Great
- ❑ Ok
- ❑ Could have been better

Activities:

Toilet: Yes / No

Lunch Time Notes:

Mood:
- ❑ Great
- ❑ Ok
- ❑ Could have been better

Lunch Eaten:

Toilet: Yes / No

Afternoon Notes:

Mood:
- ❑ Great
- ❑ Ok
- ❑ Could have been better

Activities:

Toilet: Yes / No

Messages from School:

Date:

Notes from home:

Morning Notes:

Mood:
❑ Great
❑ Ok
❑ Could have
been better

Activities:

Toilet: Yes / No

Lunch Time Notes:

Mood:
❑ Great
❑ Ok
❑ Could have
been better

Lunch Eaten:

Toilet: Yes / No

Afternoon Notes:

Mood:
❑ Great
❑ Ok
❑ Could have
been better

Activities:

Toilet: Yes / No

Messages from School:

Date:

Notes from home:

Morning Notes:

Mood:
- ❑ Great
- ❑ Ok
- ❑ Could have been better

Activities:

Toilet: Yes / No

Lunch Time Notes:

Mood:
- ❑ Great
- ❑ Ok
- ❑ Could have been better

Lunch Eaten:

Toilet: Yes / No

Afternoon Notes:

Mood:
- ❑ Great
- ❑ Ok
- ❑ Could have been better

Activities:

Toilet: Yes / No

Messages from School:

Date:

Notes from home:

Morning Notes:

Mood:
- ❑ Great
- ❑ Ok
- ❑ Could have
  been better

Activities:

Toilet: Yes / No

Lunch Time Notes:

Mood:
- ❑ Great
- ❑ Ok
- ❑ Could have
  been better

Lunch Eaten:

Toilet: Yes / No

Afternoon Notes:

Mood:
- ❑ Great
- ❑ Ok
- ❑ Could have
  been better

Activities:

Toilet: Yes / No

Messages from School:

Date:

Notes from home:

Morning Notes:

Mood:
- ❑ Great
- ❑ Ok
- ❑ Could have
  been better

Activities:

Toilet: Yes / No

Lunch Time Notes:

Mood:
- ❑ Great
- ❑ Ok
- ❑ Could have
  been better

Lunch Eaten:

Toilet: Yes / No

Afternoon Notes:

Mood:
- ❑ Great
- ❑ Ok
- ❑ Could have
  been better

Activities:

Toilet: Yes / No

Messages from School:

Date:

Notes from home:

Morning Notes:

Mood:
☐ Great
☐ Ok
☐ Could have
   been better

Activities:

Toilet: Yes / No

Lunch Time Notes:

Mood:
☐ Great
☐ Ok
☐ Could have
   been better

Lunch Eaten:

Toilet: Yes / No

Afternoon Notes:

Mood:
☐ Great
☐ Ok
☐ Could have
   been better

Activities:

Toilet: Yes / No

Messages from School:

Date:

Notes from home:

Morning Notes:

Mood:
- ❑ Great
- ❑ Ok
- ❑ Could have been better

Activities:

Toilet: Yes / No

Lunch Time Notes:

Mood:
- ❑ Great
- ❑ Ok
- ❑ Could have been better

Lunch Eaten:

Toilet: Yes / No

Afternoon Notes:

Mood:
- ❑ Great
- ❑ Ok
- ❑ Could have been better

Activities:

Toilet: Yes / No

Messages from School:

Date:

Notes from home:

Morning Notes:

Mood:
- ❑ Great
- ❑ Ok
- ❑ Could have been better

Activities:

Toilet: Yes / No

Lunch Time Notes:

Mood:
- ❑ Great
- ❑ Ok
- ❑ Could have been better

Lunch Eaten:

Toilet: Yes / No

Afternoon Notes:

Mood:
- ❑ Great
- ❑ Ok
- ❑ Could have been better

Activities:

Toilet: Yes / No

Messages from School:

Date:

Notes from home:

Morning Notes:

Mood:
- ❑ Great
- ❑ Ok
- ❑ Could have been better

Activities:

Toilet: Yes / No

Lunch Time Notes:

Mood:
- ❑ Great
- ❑ Ok
- ❑ Could have been better

Lunch Eaten:

Toilet: Yes / No

Afternoon Notes:

Mood:
- ❑ Great
- ❑ Ok
- ❑ Could have been better

Activities:

Toilet: Yes / No

Messages from School:

Date:

Notes from home:

Morning Notes:

Mood:
- ❑ Great
- ❑ Ok
- ❑ Could have been better

Activities:

Toilet: Yes / No

Lunch Time Notes:

Mood:
- ❑ Great
- ❑ Ok
- ❑ Could have been better

Lunch Eaten:

Toilet: Yes / No

Afternoon Notes:

Mood:
- ❑ Great
- ❑ Ok
- ❑ Could have been better

Activities:

Toilet: Yes / No

Messages from School:

Date:

Notes from home:

Morning Notes:

Mood:
- ❑ Great
- ❑ Ok
- ❑ Could have
  been better

Activities:

Toilet: Yes / No

Lunch Time Notes:

Mood:
- ❑ Great
- ❑ Ok
- ❑ Could have
  been better

Lunch Eaten:

Toilet: Yes / No

Afternoon Notes:

Mood:
- ❑ Great
- ❑ Ok
- ❑ Could have
  been better

Activities:

Toilet: Yes / No

Messages from School:

Date:

Notes from home:

Morning Notes:

Mood:
- ❑ Great
- ❑ Ok
- ❑ Could have been better

Activities:

Toilet: Yes / No

Lunch Time Notes:

Mood:
- ❑ Great
- ❑ Ok
- ❑ Could have been better

Lunch Eaten:

Toilet: Yes / No

Afternoon Notes:

Mood:
- ❑ Great
- ❑ Ok
- ❑ Could have been better

Activities:

Toilet: Yes / No

Messages from School:

Date:

Notes from home:

Morning Notes:

Mood:
- ❑ Great
- ❑ Ok
- ❑ Could have been better

Activities:

Toilet: Yes / No

Lunch Time Notes:

Mood:
- ❑ Great
- ❑ Ok
- ❑ Could have been better

Lunch Eaten:

Toilet: Yes / No

Afternoon Notes:

Mood:
- ❑ Great
- ❑ Ok
- ❑ Could have been better

Activities:

Toilet: Yes / No

Messages from School:

Date:

Notes from home:

Morning Notes:

Mood:
- ❑ Great
- ❑ Ok
- ❑ Could have been better

Activities:

Toilet: Yes / No

Lunch Time Notes:

Mood:
- ❑ Great
- ❑ Ok
- ❑ Could have been better

Lunch Eaten:

Toilet: Yes / No

Afternoon Notes:

Mood:
- ❑ Great
- ❑ Ok
- ❑ Could have been better

Activities:

Toilet: Yes / No

Messages from School:

Printed in Great Britain
by Amazon

46559134R00056